The
Xenophobe's Guide to
The French

Nick Yapp
Michel Syrett

RAVETTE PUBLISHING

Published by Ravette Publishing Limited
P.O. Box 296
Horsham
West Sussex RH13 8FH

Telephone: (01403) 711443
Fax: (01403) 711554

First printed 1993
Reprinted 1994
Updated 1995
Reprinted 1996
Updated 1997

Series Editor – Anne Tauté

Cover – Jim Wire, Quantum
Printer – Cox & Wyman Ltd.
Production – Oval Projects Ltd.

Xenophobe's™ and
Xenophobe's Guides™
are Trademarks.

An Oval Project
for Ravette Publishing.

Grateful thanks are given to
Michael England for his
help and information.

Contents

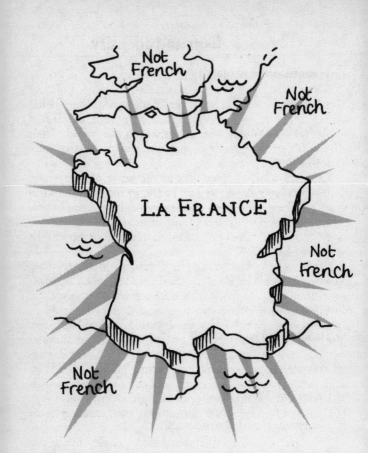

'The French see brilliance in everything they do, and French statesmen from the Renaissance to de Gaulle and on to Chirac have likened France herself to a shining light. Their own role in relation to the rest of the world borders on the Messianic.'

The French population is just over 57 million (compared with 39 million Spanish; 48 million English; 57 million Italians, and 80 million Germans).

Nationalism and Identity

Forewarned

The French care about what really matters in life – being French. They are convinced of their corporate, moral and individual superiority over all others in the world. Their charm is that they don't despise the rest of us: they pity us for not being French.

The notion of 'la force' lies at the heart of everything the French have done, well or badly, in the last thousand years or more. La force is their sense of the essence of life. It is bound up with other grand ideas such as 'la gloire', and 'la patrie', feminine words that speak of boundless stores of energy.

The French are attracted to all things vibrant, alive, moving, irresistible. Beneath their chic and natty appearances they respond to atavistic and primitive impulses.

Where most other nations would be enraged or appalled at the notion of the thinly veiled body of Marianne (the symbol of the Republic on their francs and stamps) leaping over the barricades, musket in hand, the French are moved to tears of real patriotism. The cockerel may well be their national symbol – a colourful bird which makes a great deal of noise, chases off all rivals and lays no eggs – but they never forget that their country is *la* France.

They are a public, unembarrassed people, made for special occasions – banquets, weddings, festivals, fêtes. Here they perform, happy in their roles and the overall production. In their homes, they are too cabined, cribbed, confined. The settings in which they are best seen are offices, restaurants, airport lounges (who else looks good in these?), opera houses, grands boulevards. They may sometimes behave badly, but they always act superbly.

How They See Themselves

The French see themselves as the only truly civilised people in the world, with a duty to lead and illuminate the world with their certainties.

On anything that matters the French consider themselves experts. Anything in which they're not experts, doesn't matter.

The French see glory in what others regard as defeat. Since they have won almost every war they have entered, they assume that the final battle must have resulted in a French victory, and therefore wonder why the British named Waterloo Station after a battle they lost.

They also see honour in seduction, triumph in a well-cooked entrecôte, and world supremacy in a bottle of *grand cru*. Not for nothing was Louis XIV called *Le Roi Soleil*, for the French see brilliance in everything they do, and French statesmen from the Renaissance to de Gaulle and on to Chirac have likened France herself to a shining light. Their own role in relation to the rest of the world borders on the Messianic.

How They See Others

To give their own feeling of superiority some validity, the French are generously prepared to accept that other nations have to exist.

But do not expect the French to be 'politically correct' in anything they do. They are racist, chauvinistic and xenophobic, though they smile rather than frown at other nations.

They see the English as small-minded, uncultured, faintly ridiculous, dressing badly, and spending most of their time gardening, playing cricket and drinking thick, sweet, warm beer in pubs. Yet they remain curious about them.

The English are also untrustworthy. To the French, the evacuation of the British forces from Dunkirk in 1940 was 'lâche' (cowardly), despite the fact that as many Frenchmen as possible were also rescued.

They may refer to English day-trippers to Calais as 'les fuck-offs' and regard the British generally as 'perfide' (because the French jury is still out on the little matter of whether or not Napoleon was poisoned while on St. Helena), but after one glass of Scottish malt whisky, much is forgiven.

The French no longer hate the Germans, but they aren't fond of them. They feel the Germans have a markedly inferior culture although they are happy to allow them industrial supremacy.

They also feel politically superior to the Germans, who lost all international 'presence' when they were stripped of their colonies after the First World War. The French may no longer own much of the world, but French law, language and culture persist in every continent – from Canada to the New Hebrides, from Indo-China to French Guiana, from the Ivory Coast to the Lebanon.

However uncomfortable they find the thought, the French have much in common with the Germans: a sense of formality, a reserve, a concept of racial purity, a belief in an historical destiny.

The French think the Spanish are proud but noisy, and produce more wine than is healthy for the vineyards of the Midi (Spanish wine may be sub-standard to the taste-buds of the French, but 'ça existe' – an ominous phrase).

The exceptions to this admiring-despising axis are the Belgians and the Swiss. The Swiss are objects of merciless satire in French television commercials. They may be hospitable but they are obsessively clean, and speak

French in a most odd fashion.

Valuing style in everything they do, the French have nothing but contempt for the Belgians whom they see as universally dull and totally lacking in finesse. To the French, the Belgians have always been 'thick', and they are the butt of an endless stream of French jokes, e.g:

> Two Belgian soldiers are sleeping under a tree.
> Suddenly a terrible rumbling sound awakes them.
> 'Hell and death,' says the first. 'A storm!'
> 'No,' says the other, 'those are bombs.'
> 'Thank God for that,' says the first. 'I'm terrified of thunder.'

A little envy has crept into these jokes now that the French realize the Belgians have a better standard of living than they do.

Special Relationships

Politically, the French are happy for their leaders, of whatever party, to proclaim 'l'Europe, c'est moi!' They see the European Community as unnecessary, but, if it has to exist, it is most certainly a French creation, the work of Jean Monnet (visionary and brandy distiller) in the early 1950s.

Let other Community members (especially the Germans) put up the money; the French will say how it should be spent, will give 'the Club' its cultural identity.

Historically, the French have had a love/hate relationship with the United States and Canada, having owned much of the former and populated much of the latter. But complications have arisen.

When a French-Canadian film is shown at a French cinema it has to have subtitles since the French cannot understand the soundtrack, their accent is so different. And, though the French have long admired the Americans – for their constitution, their legal system, and the fact that they, too, kicked out the British – they do not admire their American-ness.

The French have successfully persuaded generation after generation of Americans to fall in love with them, without reciprocating that love.

How Others See Them

The trouble with the French, in the eyes of many, is that they are inconsistent. This is because others fail to see that the French decide all big issues on the basis of self-interest, a feature of peasant ideology.

They regard consistency as boring, and to be boring is inexcusable.

This trait is to be seen in all aspects of French life. French women believe in feminism, but not at the price of femininity. The French produce the most beautiful paintings in the world and the ugliest wallpaper. They work hard, but are never to be seen working. Drive through France at any time of the day, week, month or year and 95% of the country appears to be uninhabited or fast asleep.

How They Would Like Others to See Them

Since the French are so convinced of their superiority, they don't really care how others see them.

Character

The Essential Frenchman

It is every Frenchman's secret wish to be Cyrano de Bergerac, the braggart, swaggering hero of Edmond Rostand's novel. Cyrano, like d'Artagnan, was a Gascon: sensitive about his appearance yet able to crush anyone who laughed at him; a great swordsman, but also a poet of infinite tenderness; a passionate lover, yet one who died of the greatest unrequited love in all literature; a man who failed, but failed gloriously. What perhaps most endears Cyrano to all Frenchmen is that he died maintaining his *panache*.

It is every Frenchman's overt wish to be Gérard Depardieu. Casting him as Cyrano in the 1991 film was a stroke of genius, for Depardieu is one of a long line of French stars (Edith Piaf, Yves Montand et *les autres*) who have risen from gutter to glitter. The French love their heroes and heroines, real or fictional, to have had a past that is depraved, deprived or delinquent – an outsider who forces his or her way in.

They love Depardieu for what he does off-screen, for who he really is, a complete turnabout from the old Hollywood system where the screen image of the star was idolised. Depardieu is a man first, a film star second – the man who turned down a film role because the harvest was due in his vineyard; the man who says had he been a woman he would have made love with director Ridley Scott; the man who is called 'a force of nature'.

Faddishness

The French, being experimental, are the most faddish people in the world. It is ingrained in their character.

being experimental, it is ingrained in their character. Nothing is so perfect that it cannot be messed with; nowhere is so beautiful that it cannot be despoiled. It's not the practical end of the road they're interested in, but the journey, the possibilities.

They love ideas, concepts, innovations – playing around with things, like democracy, nuclear energy, railway systems, gadgets.

What matters is being up-to-date. They will happily accept the hard sell if they think the paint on the product is still wet. They do not share the British cynicism about product advertising. The British admire the advertisement but don't buy the product, whereas the French don't value the advertisement as an art form in itself, but throw themselves headlong at the product.

They love to feel that life is fast moving, energetic, stylish, fashionable. They love the latest clothes, the latest slang, the latest films, the latest gadgets, but 'latest' lasts only a few days and then it's on to the newest latest. Not for nothing is *passé* a French concept.

At one extreme this results in an elitist technocracy; at the other in obnoxious cults, such as that of the '*Dûr-Être*' baby ('It's hard to be a baby'), where hordes of teenage girls mimic the words of the pop song and wander about with babies' dummies dangling at their necks.

As in everything they do, the French see-saw constantly between the sublime and the ridiculous.

Self-Image

Intellectually and spiritually the French still associate themselves very much with the land, romanticising rural and village life to wild improbabilites. Inside every

11

heart of a genuine *paysan*.

To the displaced urban French, the burly farmer – gunning down the local squirrels, fattening fettered geese for foie gras, pickling his own liver with rough cider – can be forgiven all he does, whether it's throwing up barricades of old tractors, rioting, lobbing stones at the police or (especially) burning English lambs alive.

Even as they fume at the wheels of their Peugeots and Renaults, caught in the traffic jams caused by such actions, the French feel deep empathy and spiritual communion with the culprits.

From this rustic base, the French have assumed the intellectual high ground. Post-industrial Britain, Germany, Japan and the United States have concerned themselves solely with the seedy business of making money. The French, meanwhile, have been the font and saviours of European culture – the only culture worth having.

Fifty-five Million Philosophers

To the French it is important to be seen as 'sérieux', a serious person; earnest discussion rages to and fro in France on every subject from literature to liberty, from privilege to privacy.

The French examine every facet of modern life through a philosophical microscope. In 1992, the entire population was sent copies of the Maastricht Treaty before voting in the referendum. And they read them.

This preoccupation with perceptions and conceptions makes the French much harder to govern than the Germans, who have a natural tendency towards acceptance of authority, or the English, who will grumble but do as they're told.

In the whole Western world there exists the problem of unemployment. To the Americans, Spanish, Dutch, Danes Italians, British, Germans, and Belgians it is exactly that – a problem of unemployment. To the French it is 'a question of civilization'.

At their word processors from Nantes to Nancy, from Cannes to Calais, budding philosophers are tapping away, formulating new theories, new conceits. All over France fifty five million philosophers are hungrily waiting.

Beliefs and Values

Despite a past littered with revolutions and upheavals, the French have maintained a stable and unchanging outlook on what matters in life. They have a high regard for the intellect, for qualifications and for the products of certain academic institutions.

For, although there are remnants of the old class system among the French (a few aristocrats whose forbears were not pruned by Madame la Guillotine), France is above all else a meritocracy.

In the United States the belief is that anyone can do anything if they really want to. In Britain the belief is anyone can do anything if they prove that they are able to. In France the belief is that anyone can do anything that they are qualified to do, and must be allowed to do this unchallenged, once they have proved that they went through the right channels, observed the right formalities.

The French are brain-driven. Everything they respect and hold dear is the product of the intellect and the senses. They worship ideas and those who generate them. This gives French politicians at every level a chance to come up with bold, imaginative, costly and silly projects which will receive widespread approval even when they become disastrous failures, simply because they were originally so bold, imaginative, etc.

In the 1980s the French began excitedly prospecting for oil beneath Paris. One has to admire such wild and terrifying aspirations.

They have the courage to experiment, fail, and then experiment again – not a nation burdened by its past, but one which revels in its ability to use the present as a springboard into the future.

A Passion for Roots

France and Great Britain have roughly the same size population. France is just over twice as big. This is why that feeling of space greets every visitor to France. There is plenty of room for everyone.

But the French don't see it that way. They feel there is not enough land to go round. Not only is there an undercurrent of resentment that immigrants are taking up houses, flats and jobs, there is festering resentment about the possession of every ditch, manure heap or nettle patch in the entire country.

Land – the ownership thereof – is the one bone of contention which can shatter family loyalties and general bonhomie. *Jean de Florette* and *Manon des Sources* were no figments of Pagnol's imagination. Gérard Depardieu blew himself up in the former and Daniel Auteuil hanged himself in the latter because of a feud about the ownership of land. Every French citizen would understand and empathise with the characters in both films.

The one lasting achievement of the French Revolution, in their eyes, was that it gave the land to the people, and no scheming cousin from over the hill is going to take it away.

The exception to all this is, of course, the sale of unwanted plots of land to the perfidious English with their crazy desires to buy every ruined barn and pigsty from Roscoff to Rocamadour. It's one thing to be cheated out of a pebble or two by a blood relative; it's quite another thing to fleece a total stranger, and a foreign one at that.

There may well be enough land to go round – theoretically. In practice there can never be enough, not if the population were to be halved or quartered. Without the slightest compunction, a French farmer will kill his brother, uncle, aunt, niece and nephew for a clod or two of soil. He will coax the deeds to land from his own grandmother and then lock her up for life in a smelly outhouse if it means he gets sufficient earth to plant one more row of beans.

Class and the Bourgeoisie

Being bourgeois is not so much a status as a way of life; one which manages at one and the same time to delight and disgust the French. What they like about being bourgeois is the security, the lack of vulgarity, the reliability, the continuity of life. What they detest is the predictability, the lack of curiosity, the respectability. It is an inner conflict which they have so far been unable to resolve.

On the surface all is bold égalité – imagine a customer in an English restaurant calling a waiter 'sir'. But beneath the surface old divisions remain. There are few working class lawyers, professors, doctors or accountants. It is still extremely difficult for the son of a car worker to become an architect, and even harder for his daughter.

The bourgeoisie is divided into different classes:

The *grande* bourgeoisie comes from what other countries would call 'good families', with known names – de Gaulle was a typical example. They played a great part in France's great past.

The *bonne* bourgeoisie are scions of a younger breed, far more likely to play a great part in France's great future.

The *petite* bourgeoisie are dismissed with the greatest contempt because they haven't played a great part in France's great past and they probably won't be allowed to play a great part in France's great future, and anyway their ranks are constantly being infiltrated by the great workers.

What the French do about this ambiguous state of affairs is what they do best – they ignore it, not so much in the hope that it will go away, but in the expectation that it will not matter.

The French nobility, what's left of it, has long been ignored. It hasn't gone away. It still holds regular cocktail parties, banquets, and balls, that are both lavish and secretive, but nobody takes any notice. It even holds fox hunts, but the French do not bestir themselves to sabotage such actions. Better to ignore than oppose.

It's difficult to distinguish one bourgeois from another: the grande bourgeoisie are impeccably dressed at all times and don't speak to anyone outside their own class; the bonne bourgeoisie are impeccably dressed and speak to everyone; the petite bourgeoisie are impeccably dressed and speak only to complain, so it is better not to call anyone French 'bourgeois'.

The grande bourgeoisie know they're grande bourgeoisie and won't thank you for stating the obvious. The bonne bourgeoisie will worry that they are being lumped with the petite bourgeoisie and will be insulted. It's best to ignore the entire notion.

Snobbery

The French are great snobs. They are snobbish about the dogs they own, clinging to breeds which have long passed out of fashion in Britain (cocker spaniels and 'scotties' are still chic in France). They are snobbish about where they live; they are snobbish about what they wear; they are snobbish about schools.

Few French children go to boarding schools, but there are a number of prestigious schools in France which lead on to the higher echelons of society. A child who goes to the 'right' lycée in Paris may proceed to the National Administration School or the Polytechnic School and thence to the upper strata of the civil service (known as Grand Corps d'Etat), the sort of title that would be unthinkable in state-hating Britain.

All French Presidents have graduated from these colleges. There are those, notably Giscard d'Estaing, who have graduated from all three and joined a very powerful old-boy network.

They are snobbish about where they shop, eat, play tennis, take dancing lessons, holiday, and go to church (the 10% that do attend Mass).

What makes French snobbery a little easier to accept is that it is based on good taste rather than on an hereditary principle of certain things being right.

Style

The French are a sensual people; they make love with passion; they write music that sounds like the sun rising out of the sea.

Who else would take seven and a half minutes to wrap a small 'tarte aux cerises' – putting it in a box, tying it with ribbon and handing it to the customer as though it were a new born baby – when the blessed thing is going to be consumed the moment it's taken out of the pâtisserie?

Nor is food an exception to the rule that fashion dictates everything. Nouvelle cuisine is the apotheosis of art in cooking; tiny pieces of food in a beautiful pattern – food for the eye rather than for the stomach – a triumph of style over substance.

Feminism and Femininity

French women still look as though they expect doors to be opened for them, cases to be carried, seats to be vacated. They present themselves as elegant creatures who need men in the way that a perfect jewel needs the proper setting. It is still perfectly acceptable to compliment a French woman in a way that would rile her English or American sisters.

They too demand equal pay, equal access to the top jobs, equal opportunities in work and education – that is logical, reasonable, sensible. But they have not the slightest wish to surrender the power that they have traditionally wielded so subtly, whether as good wives or good mistresses.

They still want to be wooed and seduced. The idea of hating men or wishing to exist without them seems ridiculous to the vast majority of French women. What is the point of flaunting fashion or flair if men aren't around to admire? Where is the fun or frisson in life if men aren't around to play their part?

This approach is perfectly acceptable to most French men, who are as excited by women's brains as they are by women's bodies. Madame de Pompadour and Madame de Maintenon might not have been pin ups, but they knew how to run the country better than their royal lovers. The ideal combination for a Frenchman is *mens sexy in corpore sexy*.

Wealth and Success

The moneyed French keep a much lower profile than their English, Italian, German or American counterparts. They wear dark suits, drive dark cars, live in dark houses, drink dark wine and meet in dark corners.

On the few occasions when they emerge into the light of day, they do not trot along to Champion or Intermarché. They do not frequent public transport. They (and the farmers) are the only French people who do not spend their holidays in camp sites; there are still vast, dark villas in totally untrendy resorts where all is tranquillity and gracious living.

Let others flaunt their riches in vulgar displays of jewellery, fast cars and fat cigars, the wealthy French will have none of that. They prefer to live quietly in elegant houses in discreet arrondissements, surrounded by high creeper-covered walls and protected by *chiens méchants* (the French are very honest when it comes to labelling vicious dogs – where others describe such beasts as 'guard dogs', the French are willing to admit openly that these

19

animals are 'spiteful', 'nasty', 'wicked').

This modest approach to affluence is a far cry from the ostentation of the aristos of old. Gone are the châteaux, the parks, the glittering balls and the annual horse-whipping of the peasants. Since they are almost never to be seen in public, their superiority has to be administered quickly and subtly on the few occasions when they come across the bourgeois or the Bolshevik. They do not sneer at those who cannot afford the very best, they simply affect not to understand them.

Get into a conversation with two very wealthy French men or women (it's difficult, but it can be done if there's a run on taxis on a wet day in the Rue de Rivoli) and within seconds they will turn to each other, as if to say: "It is not possible for me to understand what is being said here. Is it possible for you to understand what is being said here?" The effect is withering.

French Cars

There is little value in a second-hand French car. This is why there are no second-hand car salesmen to be found in Reims, Lyon or Marseille.

When the French buy a new car, they buy it for life – which means about three years in the case of the car and rather less in the case of too many drivers. French roads are littered with slaughter, even though they have always favoured small, rather timid looking cars. They do so partly because such cars are brave – ascending any sort of gradient is a major battle against great odds – and partly because small cars are cheaper to tax than big cars (cars are taxed according to their horsepower). There are, therefore, few luxury French limousines.

Although not made any more, the darling of all French cars is still the 2CV, which would look more at home on the end of a pole on a fairground roundabout, but which is economical, surprisingly comfortable (except when it brakes or goes round a corner), amazingly reparable, and which (significantly) the French call 'the world's most intelligent car.'

This is the sort of phrase that would take a copywriter an entire lifetime to dream up, but it comes naturally to the French because they look for intelligence in everything that moves.

Behaviour

The French are a formal people, rigid in their thinking and much of their behaviour. From Napoleon's time onwards they have always loved codes, the stricter, the better: of etiquette, fashion, ethics, diplomacy, art, literature and law.

They believe intensely in what they call *le droit*: that everything that matters should be done in the right way and in the right place and at the right time.

What they don't like, and ignore at their discretion, are petty regulations – about parking, smoking, driving, hygiene, and where you may and may not urinate.

To the French, there is a world of difference between rules and formalities. The former are to be ignored, the latter strictly observed.

This is exemplified by the elaborate way they sign off their letters. Where the English and Americans are happy to scrawl 'best wishes', 'all the best', 'write soon', or (at their most formal) 'yours faithfully', the French insist on

'Nous vous prions d'agréer, Monsieur, l'assurance de nos sentiments respecteux' ('We beg you to believe in the assurance of our respectful sentiments'), or (at their most informal) 'N'oublie pas de nous donner de tes nouvelles de temps en temps, s'il te plaît' ('Please let us have any news…').

Language is seen as embodying dignity, so language has been formalised for its own protection. French dictionaries even contain pages of phrases to be used as 'The Mechanics of Argument'.

Being stylised is as important as having style.

The Family

The French are very attached to the family – blood is definitely thicker than mineral water. They take pride in their children, partly because for many years France suffered a declining birth-rate – indeed, their defeat in the Second World War has been attributed (by them) to the simple fact that the Germans bred more successfully than they did in the first couple of decades of the 20th century. There are still tax incentives available in France to encourage and reward having a large family.

The elderly are given respect, the young are given affection. There is an interdependence in French families, where grandparents, aunts and uncles may well live very near the immediate family. All generations are included in family plans, holidays, discussions, meals and celebrations.

Children are encouraged to air their thoughts at a tender age, so that they are often good conversationalists by the time they are seven or eight years old. One of the delights of French life is the spectacle of an entire family of three or four generations all enjoying themselves at the same fête, in the same restaurant, or at a party. And one of the most severe sanctions which can be imposed is to be banned from such a function.

One French family whose son committed some mild breach of family etiquette ceremoniously removed his place setting at the table for dinner that evening, frighteningly reminiscent of poor Dreyfus* being marched round the parade ground, having the buttons torn from his uniform and his sword snapped in half. But the son uncomplainingly did as he was told and ate alone in the kitchen.

Children

English children look like devils and behave like devils. Italian children look like fallen angels and behave like fallen devils. French children look like angels and behave like devils.

Watch any group of beautifully groomed and attired French tots on the beach or in the park, and, the moment all grown-up backs are turned, see the mud or sand stuffed into eyes and ears, hear the thud of spade or boot on knee, thrill to the fusillade of stones or gravel as one angel pelts another.

This is because anarchy sets in when French children are let off the lead. They are at their bourgeois best hand-in-hand with an adult (mama, papa, grandmère, au pair, nanny) in formal, structured settings: a fête, a family party, an outing. The sight of a crocodile of thirty or

*Captain Dreyfus, whose wrongful conviction and deportation to Devil's island in 1894 (for supposedly giving away military secrets to Germany), outraged and divided French opinion.

forty French children, marching hand-in-hand in pairs, is as enchanting as it is still commonplace.

On being introduced to an adult, they shake hands solemnly, or offer their cheek to be kissed with becoming modesty and not a trace of embarrassment.

The French go to great lengths to make special provision for their children, especially at holiday time. Every beach in France has its swimming school, presided over by elderly French swimming instructors who are even thinner than French cyclists. The training is rigorous and comprehensive, but the children are seldom allowed into the water.

Next door is a supervised sports area where the little 'ducks' and 'dolphins' are taught how to climb ropes, turn somersaults and crawl through lengths of pipe by bronzed teenagers who take their responsibilities very seriously.

French children have, therefore, grown up sensing that they are most important. They have evidence of this in the grooming they receive, in the way they are included in adult conversation, in the effusive admiration that aunts and uncles, grandparents and godparents bestow upon them.

They love the way they are worshipped.

Elders

The traditional rural ways of keeping a family together are still prevalent in much of France. The idea of putting Granny into a home is anathema to the French, who see it as natural to look after their own elderly people. Besides it is so much cheaper and one always has a babysitter to hand.

Animals

In their fantasies the rural French are great and primitive hunters and therefore don't really understand why people should want to keep animals as pets.

To them, there are only two reasons for having anything to do with animals: to kill and eat them or because they are useful (sheep dogs, guard dogs, etc.)

The urban French mainly own utilitarian or display pets – an Alsatian to guard their property, or a poodle to show off their exquisite taste in à la mode accessories – but they are becoming increasingly pet conscious. There are some 10 million dogs in France, many of whom eat at table with their owners, and a frightening number of whom are allowed to accompany their owners on motorbikes.

By and large they have none of the nauseous sentimentality which the English have for animals. It would never occur to the French to have such an institution as the Battersea Dogs Home – for who would want to adopt a dog whose owners had abandoned it in the first place?

Pet dogs which trespass on to other people's land run the risk of being surreptitiously poisoned. Stray dogs are not pitied by the French. They are destroyed.

Driving

The self-centredness of the French is most apparent in the way they drive. Anarchy holds the steering wheel, and the real French character emerges. Traffic rules are regarded by the French as interesting suggestions which might be considered if one hadn't something far more important in mind.

The average French man (and woman) sits patriotically at the wheel of his Peugeot, Citroën or Renault, switches on the engine, shoves the car into gear and then drives the length and breadth of Europe as though it were a private estate.

They are not just bad drivers, they are insanely dangerous drivers. Every major road interchange is like a crowded dance floor, with cars waltzing up to each other, bumping, jostling for space, everybody knowing where they want to go and madly resenting the presence of those in the way.

One of the most exciting things to do in France is to try to use a pedestrian crossing. Those who are slow, through age or indisposition, should resign themselves to living out their days on one side of the street.

One of the first laws the German army imposed on the citizens of Paris in 1940 was that they should cross the roads only at specifically appointed places. The Third Reich was, from that moment, doomed.

The French share the Germans' belief that the English are the world's worst drivers, although the yearly carnage on French roads suggests otherwise. They drive facing sideways, backwards, upwards (if their car has a sun roof), with perverse individuality and scorn for impending disaster.

They ignore worsening road conditions with a shrug of the shoulders and a flick of the Gauloise. They have a faith in the average car's braking system which puts Joan of Arc's faith in God to shame. They regard every *feu rouge*, every *carrefour*, every *rond-point* as an affront to their individual liberty.

'Prudence' say the Warning signs at the side of French autoroutes. It's not even up for negotiation.

Standards

The French are at heart traditionalists. Though they dearly love revolutions, pulling everything down and starting from scratch (endless scope for debate and discussion), they disapprove of shifts in behaviour.

Everything must be done *comme il faut* (properly), an expression that applies equally to getting married and getting drunk, stuffing a duck and filling in a form, addressing an envelope and addressing a teacher. There is an established order of things, and the order was established by the French.

The desire to maintain standards is best seen on any holiday in the summer. Where the British, the Spanish, the Italians and even the Germans relax sufficiently to let a little stubble grow, or mealtimes become irregular, or dress become bizarre and ill co-ordinated, the French behave as though they were still under the microscope of real life.

French men and women take two hours over their morning toilette. Watch any Frenchman at a camp site in the summer and see how long he spends shaving, trimming his moustache, and generally abluting. By the time he has finished, it is the hour of the apéritif.

Wives cook three course luncheons which they serve to their husbands in the sweltering heat at little tables with linen napkins and polished cutlery. The white wine stands in an ice bucket in what little shade there is; the red wine is chambré-ed in the tent. Everything is correct – the bread, the cheese, the sauce.

Monsieur eats greedily. Madame stands behind him, and a little to the side, nodding happily. She will do the washing-up immediately the meal is finished. All will be neat and tidy before any other activity is even considered.

27

Meanwhile, all over the rest of the camp site, foreigners are dropping food out of their hands, their mouths, their pockets.

Religion

Despite their Catholic tradition, the French have always been religious mavericks. For a hundred years or more they had their own Pope in Avignon rivalling and fighting the other Pope in Rome.

Catholicism has suited them, with its emphasis on sin and exoneration rather than guilt and shame. The notion that it's alright to sin so long as you repent afterwards fits in well with the French insistence that there must be a way round every problem.

Churches in France are heavy, dark, depressing buildings, smelling of aniseed and carbolic, presided over by priests who have lost much of the authority they used to have within the community, and who are anyway much more concerned with the collapse of Socialism than they are by the decline in Catholicism.

What the French have very cunningly done is to abandon many of the duties and burdens of religion but keep the feast days and holidays.

This is why so many foreigners are to be seen, on the Day of the Assumption of the Blessed Virgin Mary, wandering morose and penniless through the streets of towns where all the banks are shut.

It is yet another example of the French plucking the good things from life, abandoning the rest, and having no conscience at all about what happens in consequence.

Manners

The French, especially Parisians, are phenomenally rude – when they wish to be. There is none of the unthinking or forgetful rudeness of other people. When the French are rude it is because they consider that the occasion demands it.

In particular, the French are happy to be rude to people who are complete strangers. If you ring a wrong number in France, you can expect an earful of quite outrageous insults. Among friends, insults are also frequently traded, but with no permanent damage to the relationships. In England, if you insult someone, you do it for life. In France, people insult each other dreadfully one day, and act as though nothing had been said the next.

Etiquette

The French are, par excellence, a sociable people, but they value their privacy. They jealously guard their moments of meditation, their daily family discussions, their right to sit alone in a bar or café peering at a glass of Pernod while the world walks by.

They observe a strict code of etiquette and are adamant that certain things are not done in public. French men do not comb their hair in the street. Neither do French women apply their make-up. No matter how hot the day, clothes are not discarded as one promenades along the street.

The French parliament once debated at length the question as to whether or not a gentleman in a pissoir, when recognising a female passer-by, should lift his hat to her.

On the Métro and on French buses seats are reserved for those wounded in the war and pregnant women. Should some gum-chewing layabout sit in one of these seats, he will soon be asked to move by one better entitled to it who will have the manifested moral support of all the other passengers.

They respect the space of others by respecting their own space and carefully monitoring what they do within it, not so much in case someone is watching but because they assume everyone is bound to be watching. So, whereas drivers caught in an English traffic jam resort to picking their noses as a way of passing the time, drivers caught in a French traffic jam scrutinise themselves in the driving mirror, and make minor but important adjustments to their ties, hair, eyebrows or moustaches. The distinction is a question of style.

The one exception to all this is the Emptying of the Male Bladder. Frenchmen pee everywhere – by the side of the road (towards the traffic as well as away from it): into rivers, lakes and canals; against trees, shrubs and lamp-posts; behind shops, garages, railway stations. They pee while they smoke, talk, fish, garden, adjust carburettors, mix cement or walk horses.

A visitor was holidaying in France, by the sea. It was midnight. He had eaten well at the village restaurant, and drunk just enough wine to reach that point where life is infinitely good. The sea was calm, the moon was full. He was as near Paradise as he expects to be this side of the grave. And then three Frenchmen lurched out of the night and pissed in the ocean.

The reverie died instantly. But what really upset him was the cordial way all three wished him 'Bonne nuit' as they zipped up their trousers and left.

Greetings

Foreigners often fail to appreciate the formal code of greeting in France. The French shake hands with everyone (family, children, strangers), at home, on the way to work, at work, on leaving work, on the way home from work, etc. In an office that employs perhaps a dozen people, therefore, no work will be done for the first half hour while those who have not met since the day before remind each other who they are.

However, it is important to remember with whom one has shaken hands on any one day. The French regard it as extremely bad manners to shake hands twice, as though one had not taken adequate notice the first time.

It is still the custom to say 'bonjour' and 'au revoir' to one and all when entering or leaving a shop or bar. This is not because the French are excessively polite. It is because they see acknowledging the existence of others as a way of avoiding being rude.

There are those shopkeepers to whom one should say "Bonjour, monsieur", and those to whom one should say "Bonjour, monsieur. Ça va?", and those shopkeepers to whom one should say "Bonjour, monsieur. Ça va?..." and a whole lot more.

The distinction may seem unbearably subtle to others, but to the French it is most important. Manners maketh civilization to them. Without rigid formalities, the primitive would assuredly assert itself.

Kissing is not as much of a feature of French life as others suppose. But when it does take place, it must be done properly, according to the rules.

The correct order is left cheek, right cheek, left cheek – very formal, very stylised. In Paris four kisses are sometimes permitted: left, right, left, right. Woe betide the floundering foreigner who moves right where he should have moved left, or makes too intimate a contact with his mouth. The French greeting kiss, as distinct from the French Kiss, is a subtle affair.

The insistent formality of French greetings makes huge inroads into their lives. On a beach near Biarritz, eight Parisians lay down on their smart beach towels to sunbathe. Along came a ninth. All eight stood up, to shake hands with or embrace the ninth. All nine lay down. Along came a tenth. All nine stood up, to shake hands with or embrace the tenth. This went on until there were twenty-three people in the group. Very little was accomplished in the way of sunbathing.

Tu-ing and Vous-ing

One of the few things that most people learn about the French is that they have two words for 'you' – tu and vous. What nobody ever learns is when to use which.

It is perfectly polite to use 'tu' to a dog, even if you have never met him (or her) before. But it is safest not to use 'tu' to a human being until he or she does it to you, for to be 'tutoi-ed' is to be admitted into the inner sanctum of French life, to be accepted, to be granted the status of close friend.

'Tu' is not merely a grammatical form. It is an important but subtle social signal. There are some you will never say 'tu' to, not if the Foreign Legion were to take up knitting or the local boulangerie were to start selling Mother's Pride.

There are some French couples who never use 'tu' to one another in their entire married life.

Culture

It is the honest opinion of every French man and woman that France has always led the world in matters cultural – architecture, painting, music, cinema, literature, sculpture, mime, theatre, ballet, and how to die at dawn in a duel.

They may well be right, for they have always known how to make the everyday look exceptional, artistic: walking down a street, sitting at a café, reading a book. Their homes may lack some of the splendour and enthusiasm of the English and Americans (inside and out), but they are happy to be judged by the books on their shelves, the pictures on their walls, the compact discs in their music systems.

People in France fight, plot and train to reveal the breadth of their intellect. They have a name for it: *le discours*. It can mean anything from idle chatter to a speech, but their favoured use of it is as a 'piece of discursive reasoning'. Those skilled in this craft (about 95% of the population), are held in high esteem. A French man or woman will hold up a piece of nifty reasoning with the same pride that another might feel when displaying an Impressionist painting, a Fabergé egg or a Sèvres vase.

To the French, to grab the cultural high ground is to be unassailable. Clashes between intellectuals in France have all the excitement and dynamism of an international boxing match.

Cinema

Just as the French make an art form of everyday life, so they make everyday life into an art form.

Dozens of French films consist of little more than several people (bored, lonely, jealous, mad, bewildered – but mostly bored) sitting down to a lengthy and wordless meal.

In the hands of any other film-makers such oeuvres would be worthless, but somehow the French make masterpieces out of the mundane.

A French audience will watch such a film and then go to a restaurant to discuss it and relate it to their own lives. It is arguable that this has its own rationale.

The French invented the notion of the film director as auteur, as the person who stamped his image of the world on the film, and his image of the film on the world.

They have always taken their film industry seriously. In 1940 Vichy officials pronounced: "If we have lost the war it is because of *Quai des Brumes*," an archetypal French melodrama of the 1930s starring Jean Gabin and Michèle Morgan, about an army deserter who rescues a young girl from a gang of crooks, with the kind of unhappy ending that French audiences adore.

Television and Radio

French radio provides pop stations and local stations and nostalgic stations and serious music stations and sports and news stations, and gimmicky phone-in and phone-out stations, but nothing that produces the brand loyalty which exists, for example, for BBC's Radio 4 in Britain.

One of the few hugely popular radio programmes is one where the presenter phones members of the public in the hope of catching them in bizarre and embarrassing situations. A form of radio voyeurism, it provides suitable subjects for discussion since the French are obsessed with all aspects of human behaviour.

Other than this, French radio is little more than a carbon copy of the worst of American radio and is used mainly as a background when they are driving to and from work.

The best thing on French television used to be de Gaulle's frequent pleas to his fellow citizens to calm down, go home and leave everything to him. No one since has used the medium so well. Television today is only important because it shows the news (by which the French mean what is happening in France and/or what the French are doing elsewhere), sport (the Tour de France, the French rugby team, racing from Chantilly), and old French films.

For the rest, there is a rash of grim and cheap game shows watched only by the desperate, averagely awful breakfast television, and one shining light – a programme called *Apostrophes* which attracts an audience of up to six million viewers. This is the literary chat show that, at a time when he was President of France, Giscard d'Estaing took time off to take part in, to discuss the works of Guy de Maupassant.

Although facing the usual half dozen political crises at the time, the President hastily brushed up on the subject and appeared, suave, calm and (most important) erudite. The result of his labour was not the collapse of the government, but an improvement in his own standing and a sellout of de Maupassant's books throughout the country.

The problem with television is that it keeps people at home, where debate is limited in terms of participants. The older French would rather be in a bar (where most TV sport is watched) or a restaurant or a friend's house, talking about it.

Literature – from Tintin to Tartuffe

The French are devotees of the *bande dessinée*, those wonderful comic strip books which tell the adventures of Astérix, Tintin, Lucky Luke and others, and which they have raised to an art form in its own right.

Here for once they abandon their strict approach to their own tongue, and use humorous and colloquial phrases, as though taking the opportunity to indulge in all the things they're not allowed to write elsewhere.

The French glory in their long-winded literature and poetry. They especially admire Proust (novelist and manic depressive), Voltaire (humanitarian and jailbird), Verlaine (poet and debauchee), Molière (comic dramatist who was denied holy burial) and Flaubert (novelist and perfectionist, who spent hours or days on a single sentence, seeking the right word). They also admire Baudelaire, Racine, Hugo, Dumas (father and son), Rabelais, Pagnol and almost anyone who wrote in the French language.

Readers of Proust discover painfully the idea that the mind is a mass of memories and that we live our lives as servants of these memories, however firmly locked away.

In a scene in one book, the hero, who is having an illicit affair with someone, is in a hotel room, dabbing his mouth with a towel. The crispness of the towel reminds him of his childhood and a similar towel. In another scene, his teaspoon slips and the sound of it resonating against the cup reminds him of a bell in his cottage garden. All this is very French – the idea of touch, smell, sound unlocking the past and reviving fifty year-old memories.

The tragedy of Proust is that it takes twelve volumes to do this, and nobody has yet found a satisfactory way of translating the first sentence of Volume I into English.

The Press and *Paris Match*

The French have a great number of regional papers and several national daily newspapers – one for the extreme Right, one for the extreme Left, one for the Right of Centre Right, one for the Left of Centre Right, and so on.

They believe newspapers should consist of text rather than pictures, information rather than advertisements, serious matters rather than frivolous affairs. Life must be well balanced, however. The French have always been the world's finest high wire artistes, so they have their comics and the weekly *Canard Enchaîné*, a kind of French *Private Eye*.

They also have *Paris Match*, more an institution than a magazine. The French love it because it confirms all that they wish to believe about themselves, that they are smart, beautiful, clever, artistic, always in the limelight.

They don't see it in any way as exposing the faults, flaws, mistakes or weaknesses of France. If a *Paris Match* poll reveals that 71% of its readers think the French are racist, few are shocked. It is not a question of whether this is a morally good or bad result – it's a French result, and that's what matters.

Paris Match proves that the rest of the world trails after the French, picking up their leads in fashion, cinema, literature, politics, design, technology, transport, town planning and the use of garlic. That is why it has survived the onslaught of television news coverage, where *Picture Post* and others have folded.

To succeed in England, you have to be like the Germans. To succeed in Germany, you have to be like the Americans. To succeed in America, you have to be like the Japanese. To succeed in France, you have to be like the French.

Paris Match is exactly like the French.

Music

The French have managed to hold on to their traditional music. Within only a few minutes of being in France it is possible to hear the strains of piano accordion, soprano saxophone, violin, guitar and drums – the classic French ensemble. The rest of the world may have been taken over by the sounds of the U.K. and U.S., but not France.

People still sing songs about a young man and a young woman in the spring, in a park, in a fiacre, in love, just as they did a hundred years ago. All French singers have tremendous vibrato and every French song is as much a piece of drama as a piece of music.

Sense of Humour

The French have always admired physical humour and clowning, having virtually adopted both Buster Keaton and Jerry Lewis, and they admire the droll comedy of Americans like Jack Benny and George Burns.

French humour relies as much on what you don't say as what you do say. They approach a piece of verbal humour from an oblique angle, with the same subtlety that they still bring to love-making, but with a bigger laugh at the end.

They are much taken with the art of mime made famous by Marcel Marceau, and on any warm day many young men and women are to be seen in pedestrian precincts pretending to erect deck chairs, to be stuck in revolving doors, to be carrying huge panes of glass on a windy day.

No one has yet discovered why.

Leisure and Pleasure

Annual Holidays

The French are great holiday makers for they have discovered one great truth of holiday life – it is possible to get away from it all and yet take it all with you.

Long ago most French abandoned the expensive hotels in the expensive resorts and took to 'le camping' with a gusto that few others manage. All over southern Europe (the French seldom go north) their beautiful tents are to be seen: one section for living quarters, one section for sleeping quarters, one section for cooking quarters and one section as a garage and workshop.

The family takes its wine, its food, its bicycles, its recreation, and, most important, its culture with it. They eat French, they drink French, they relax French and they exercise French.

Every possible holiday location in France, including the stops on the autoroutes, has its *parcours sportif*, a 3 to 4 mile circuit strewn with exercise points. Most French under the age of fifty spend half their holiday puffing and panting their way round them, stopping every so often to drip sweat and pull a hamstring or two on the parallel bars, sit-up benches, climbing ropes and monkey runs which the local council has so kindly provided.

The heady mixture of sun, sand, sea and swooning exhaustion reaches its high saltwater mark in the Club Méditerranée – a package holiday concept which allows a baffling range of choices. Started in the 1950s by Gérard Blitz as a 'strange cocktail of la vie de château et la vie de sauvage' they offer culture, a sense of community, sport, good food and wine and a great sense of civilized adventure.

In exotic locations from Corfu to Tahiti, they give the French a chance to holiday with the French.

Other Holidays

The French have a generous helping of days off. With luck, these fall on Tuesdays or Thursdays, which enables them to take Monday or Friday off as well, and thereby create a long weekend – a practice known as faire le pont ('to make the bridge'), but it might just as well be known as faire le point.

Best of all holidays is Bastille Day, when everyone comes out on to the streets and throws fire crackers at each other in affirmation of the individual against the State.

Le Weekend

As with the holidays, so with the weekends. Large cities empty and the roads fill with traffic as the French head out into the country, either to spend a night or two in their second home, or to visit those members of the family who still live 'la vie paysanne'.

It was a long time before the French allowed themselves a workless weekend but it is now another of their obsessions. The gradual decline of the French lunch-hour has meant that the evening meal has become more important. Since this is taken between 7.30 and 9.00 little time is left to go out during the week. Therefore all sport, clubbing, dancing, visits to the cinema and the theatre tend now to be mainly weekend activities. In fact, the French cram so much into their Saturdays and Sundays that it is often quite a relief to get back to work.

Le Sport

Everything stops for the Tour de France, when the entire population lines the route, breathless for that split second when several hundred cyclists whizz past on their *vélos* in one highly coloured blur. It is the most popular sporting event in France because it's bright, it's fast, it's essentially French, and you can drink for a couple of weeks while watching it. Cycling is a mania in France.

At all times of the year, men as thin as cycle spokes hurtle up and down mountains, overtaking anything slower than a Porsche, covering hundreds of kilometres a day and living off a diet of water and adrenalin. Cycling glorifies the individual in his battle against the landscape, the elements, the odds (lorries are so much bigger), and punctures.

The French are interested in only four team games: rugby football, basketball, soccer, and, to a lesser extent, volleyball. They play all four in a thoroughly French way, with speed, élan, audacity and a lot of noise.

Sex

The French are at ease with their bodies, and this, together with their unquestioning belief in themselves, gives them considerable sex-appeal.

The young Jeanne Moreau may not have been as beautiful as Grace Kelly, but she was much sexier. Jean Gabin was certainly not as handsome as Cary Grant, but he had more sex appeal in the tilt of his hat than Grant had in his entire body.

The French have a pleasantly guileless approach to sex. In the old days they believed it was necessary for a young couple to be chaperoned. The chaperone was there not in case the couple made love, but because it was expected that they would do so. Sex has always been seen as part of life, not as an extra to the curriculum.

What distinguishes the French sexually from others is that there are still many unwritten rules regarding sex. If a man invites a girl to his apartment, she can rest assured that he will make a pass at her. To do anything less would be an insult (in the eyes of the man) to them both.

On the other hand, although a Frenchman might well make a pass at the wife of a friend or colleague, he would never make a pass at the friend or colleague's daughter.

The first is permissible, part of the wonderful nip and tuck of French life. The second is unthinkable, an abject betrayal of friendship, because the daughter is not in a position to make an informed decision.

Seduction is an art form to be practised only among equals.

Eating

For the French, enjoyment of food in a good restaurant, or in the home of a fine chef, is a spiritual experience, a neo-religious ritual.

There are still many parts of France where two hours is allowed for lunch, though more and more French people are opting for a shorter lunch-break and an earlier finish to work, so that they can get home to their families. They may then immediately go out again, en famille, to eat their evening meal, for even the humblest roadside café can offer a blanquette de veau that is every bit as good as a top class restaurant, at a fraction of the price.

They are appalled by the English practice of eating cheese after a pudding. To progress from meat to cheese is natural – savoury to savoury. To progress from pudding to cheese is like eating ice cream with roast beef. How can the British sully their palates in this way? Do they not understand the notion of complementarity? Faced with such barbarism on the part of visitors, the French have no option but to be dictatorial about food, to tell people what to eat and how to eat it.

As with everything French, food is the subject of endless discussion. At a business conference in France, two French male colleagues talked together for over half an hour, not about sport or work, but about the mushrooms they had picked during the summer and how they ate them and with what sauce. Particular stress was placed on some very rare mushrooms which one of the delegates had found on a mountainside in Corsica and on the cream sauce that had accompanied them.

On the other hand, there is a lack of refinement about some French food which others find repellent. They not only eat any and every part of an animal, they take no trouble to hide what part it is. The British and the Americans mince up the toenails, genitals, brains, tails and ears of cows, pigs and sheep, turning them into unidentifiable products called 'burgers', 'brawn', 'haslet' or 'luncheon meat'. The French call a pig's foot 'un pied de porc' and slap it on a tray with all the rest of the much-prized charcuterie.

The gibes historically hurled at the French for eating snails, frogs' legs and garlic are ineffective. The French know how to cook, serve and eat all three. Stomachs may quail at the snail, but the melted butter will be the finest in the world. Frogs' legs may seem to provide little in the way of sustenance, but they will be exquisitely arranged on the plate.

Drinking

Only the inhabitants of Luxembourg drink more than the French, who consume 15.5 litres of pure alcohol per splitting head per year.

In Normandy and Brittany vast quantities of cider pour down French throats and gurgle on to French livers – always a source of concern. Beer is popular throughout France. The wealthy are fond of whisky, especially malt whisky which has special cachet. In south west France, along the cosmopolitan coast, Gin Fizz is quaintly advertised in bars, a relic of older days. Pastis, Byrrh, and other apéritifs still have their customers.

But it is wine that makes the French world go round.

The French *know* about wine. (They should do; they imbibe, combined with water, an ever increasing amount of wine at mealtimes from a tender age.)

Whatever the Spanish, the Germans, the Australians or the Californians may say, the French know that they produce the best wine in the world. Visitors to the Museum of Wine in Bordeaux or the University of Wine at Château Suze-la-Rousse tiptoe past the exhibits with more reverence than would be seen in Notre Dame.

A family of vegetarians, invited to a meal with a French family in Bordeaux, were treated to a seven course meal, every course of which was cheese. But, there was a different bread to go with each cheese and, most importantly, a different wine to go with each duo. The meal was wonderful, each course superbly distinguished from the others; a 'grand vin' here, a 'petit vin' there. And they awoke the following morning with no after effects.

After a banquet, the French President of the Board of Trade addressed guests for a full ten minutes, not on the economy or international trade or tariffs and duties, but on the glories of the wines that had accompanied their meal. He dwelled at length on the '78 de la Tour and the '55 Sauternes. He reviewed the experience in which they had all shared, and then led the assembled gathering in an act of bibulous worship.

What is Sold Where

Both men and women in France like to make a ceremony of shopping. Where others see it as a chore, especially something as humdrum and everyday as buying food, the French turn the whole thing into a cross between a drama and a pilgrimage.

French housewives set off with their wicker baskets to visit boulangerie, poissonnerie, pâtisserie, boucherie and fruiterie. They prod, sniff, taste and generally assault whatever is on sale preparatory to buying it. To do less would be an insult to the trader. As they near their selection, an earnest discussion takes place between customer and shop-keeper, ultimately involving everyone within earshot – another of the much loved French debates. The one knows what she wants; the other knows what she should have. Eventually an agreement is reached.

The French may have the largest supermarkets in the world outside the United States (and increasingly shop in them) but they also like to make their shops as specialised as possible. It is never necessary to ask "Do you sell such-and-such?" It is obvious what any French shop sells, because it only sells one thing. Florists don't sell fruit, pharmacies don't sell sandwiches or CDs, pâtissiers don't sell bowls of soup.

The ultimate in specialisation is to be found in French butchers' shops. Here the discerning buyer has to make his or her way to shops which sell only red meat, only horse meat, only pig meat, only poultry.

To obtain the ingredients for an English steak and kidney pie could take all day.

Health and Hygiene

The French, understandably, given their eating and drinking habits, view every ailment as a by-product of liver dysfunction.

Colds, blisters, varicose veins, mumps, baldness, fallen arches – all are attributed to liver trouble. The cure for everything, therefore, is to drink more Badoît, Evian, Perrier, Vichy, St. Yorre, Vittel – to flush out the offending organ. If this fails, the entire system has to be purged, and that means employing the French panacea – suppositories. The suppository is to the French what the cup of tea is to the English, useless as a treatment, but a great comfort in time of need.

The French believe in the expert. If you have a back pain in France, you go to see a back doctor. If you have a cough, you go to a chest specialist. If you have an earache, you go to an expert on ears. (In rural areas this may pose problems, so there are large parts of France where treatment is still a matter for the wise old members of the family.)

Since no one doctor has a monopoly on a person's illnesses, diseases and debilities, each patient is the custodian of his or her own medical records, which they take around with them to any doctor they visit.

Averagely healthy citizens may, therefore, never see the same doctor twice, but they can give you chapter and verse on their medical histories, and thus have far more control over their own health and treatment.

However, unless a French person is seriously ill, he is far more likely to go to a pharmacist than to a doctor. The pharmacist listens to the customer's self-diagnosis and then suggests what pills or potions should be taken.

The work and effects of these drugs will be carefully described in great detail and the dosage recorded in clear, neat handwriting on the label. It is impossible to nip into a chemist's in France for a couple of painkillers without getting a complete run-down on The Work of the Aspirin.

Hygiene

The French are not afraid of normal body odours – such smells they regard as natural. They have a saying 'don't be afraid of the microbes'. They regard the American obsession with hygiene as prissy. A French family of four uses only one bar of soap a month.

To their minds, to cover up the stench of the body with deodorants is to make a pathetic attempt to defy the force of nature. The smell of a hot human being is a natural aphrodisiac to the French. They associate the smell as part of the overall sexual experience. A foreigner travelling in a crowded train from Paris to Nice in August may not share this view.

It is not for nothing that the French are the world's leading parfumiers – Guerlain, Lancôme, Christian Dior, Chanel, Madame Rochas. They see nothing incompatible in this. It is one thing to worship the smell of the human body and quite another to make billions of francs a year out of small phials of liquid which attempt to disguise it.

Systems

There is neither time nor place for the mediocre in the lives of the French. Services must be either useless (grounds for complaint and argument, and possibly revolution) or excellent (grounds for sustained paeans of self-congratulation).

After limping along with a quaint and romantic telephone system for fifty years, the French decided they wanted a modern one in 1970, and by 1980 they had one of the best in the world. 'France Telecom' fits phones about five minutes after they're ordered, and sends bills which itemise the date, the number, the time, the duration of the call and the cost. It cannot be long before they also supply a transcript of the conversation.

Transport

The French, who are habitually late themselves, abhor lateness in public transport. If a train is two minutes late arriving at the most remote station in the Republic, testy phone calls are made up and down the line, and someone's peaked cap of authority is held up to ridicule.

If a bus is late the indignant passengers expect to be told why and are quite prepared to debate the strengths and weaknesses of the driver's excuse right there on the spot, even though it makes the bus even later.

This obsession with punctuality can cause problems for passengers on the high speed train, the 'TGV'. As the train approaches a station, the conductor tells passengers how long the train will stop for, and this time is meticulously adhered to. It is thus a common sight on major French stations to see the automatic doors of the TGV closing before all descending passengers have got off and long before all ascending passengers have got on.

What is undeniable is that the French very sensibly made their country exactly the right size and shape for railways – medium large, and square. There is none of the 'going-sideways' problems imposed on British railways by the predominantly vertical shape of the country. There are none of the problems of size which bedevil Canadian, Russian or American railways where distances are so vast that a plane is bound to be a quicker method of travel. So the French have their TGV and their world records. It is fair and correct to expect the best and be furiously disappointed if it isn't forthcoming.

Although admitting that they have a role to play in allowing private, commercial and visiting vehicles to move about France, the French see their roads primarily as a means of connecting one town of great cultural and historical importance with a neighbouring town (of similar importance). This enables mayors and other civic dignitaries easy access to each other for receptions, dinners, wine tastings.

Brown signs beside all the autoroutes warn drivers not of approaching junctions or hazards, but of approaching pine forests, oyster beds, châteaux, geese farms and mountains. Multi-coloured signs on all main roads warn drivers of approaching hotels, swimming pools, tennis courts, restaurants and historic churches. The French believe that, in order to arrive, one must travel hopefully.

France has far more internal air routes than are needed. Some of the routes are so short that there's scarcely time to tell passengers what action to take in anticipation of 'an emergency' (their word for a crash).

If time allows, however, they consider it essential to serve champagne on the flight, so that if there were to be a crash at least it would happen in style.

Education

The problems of attempting to change the education system in France reveal an essential truth about the French – you can change the superstructure, but you can't change the way people behave.

After the riots of 1968 all but the most diehard agreed that changes had to be made. A whole series of reforms were embarked on: mixed ability classes, an end to the separation of the academically gifted into special schools, more informality in teacher/pupil relationships.

None of it worked because the main aim of all these reforms was 'a new Republican idealism', no different from the old Republican idealism. All that happened was that standards allegedly dropped.

The Government didn't mind about the worsening of standards in mathematics, science and technology, but it took a poor view of a drop in standards of knowledge of history (the story of France) and literature (the stories of France). The only popular educational reform during some twenty years was the creation of councils in all secondary schools – democratic governing boards composed of parents, pupils, teachers, Ministry officials and local bigwigs. These have fed the French hunger for debate without achieving anything.

The battle in French education has always been to wrest control from central government. Until the 1980s it was necessary to get Ministerial permission from Paris to hold a student dance in Grenoble or Bordeaux or Toulouse or any other French university.

Some independence has been won. Today, despite the imposition of a national curriculum which ensures that every French child everywhere covers identical ground, French schools are permitted to decide for themselves how to spend 10% of their teaching time. They tend not to. It is the old, old story of the French shedding blood and laying down their lives to gain some essential freedom and then not knowing what to do with it.

French schools and universities are big. So big that two teachers once met on holiday and were amazed to discover that they taught at the same school. But this is not so surprising because education for teachers and pupils is very much a nose-to-the-grindstone affair.

All that matters is the famous *baccalauréat*, their end of school examination, the greatest French obsession of all time. Parents are prepared to lie, bribe, cheat so that their children succeed in 'le bac'.

It is the essential qualification, for those who pass have proved that they are cultured, and those who fail are considered little better than the Americans.

Law

This is yet another example of the French adherence to logic and discussion as a means of structuring life. The entire French legal system is based on an arbitrational rather than an adversarial model.

In any legal dispute it is not a question of proving one side right and the other wrong, it is a question of arriving at the truth.

In property deals, one lawyer can act for both buyer and seller because his or her role is simply to make sure that the deal is conducted fairly and legally. The lawyer is not there to help either side win, or to extort more money from the buyer, or to persuade the seller to drop the price (though he or she may suggest either of these moves if the deal is proving difficult). The system is based instead on the assumptions that:

a) we are all reasonable people
b) we all know what we want from this deal
c) dishonesty is not on the agenda.

The French hold fast to these assumptions despite massive evidence to the contrary on all three counts.

Crime and Punishment

The French police in whatever form – gendarmes, CRS (riot police), national police – have an unchallenged and widely held reputation for being tough, vain and heavily corrupt. So the French are not shocked when this is proved to be the case.

The average gendarme is more concerned with fighting paperwork than fighting crime. Thus tax evasion, illicit gambling, black-market dealing, petty theft and vagrancy are 'not serious' enough to sully the records, but they make exceptions to this rule for serious matters such as rape, murder, arson and assault.

Occasionally nothing is worth bothering about. In a tiny gendarmerie in a little village in south west France some days the local gendarmes play marbles or boules; at other times they listen to dance music or blow up balloons for their children.

Every day they close the gendarmerie for two hours at lunchtime, while delicious smells waft from the kitchen at the back. Every evening they are to be seen sipping their apéritifs on the verandah.

If you knock on their door to report a mugging, they are much put out, but helpfully give you the phone number of the gendarmerie in St. Jean de Luz, a few miles away. The locals are not in the least disturbed by any of this.

It would be a mistake, however, to underestimate the French police. If they take a dislike to you, they can hold you in the cells for up to 24 hours without bringing any charge. This is known as 'detained under surveillance'.

The French are about as criminal as the English and far less so than the Americans. But every nation has its own criminal speciality. The French do like larceny and murder.

They have a very low rate for attempted murder and a high rate for successfully concluded murder. It seems that when a French man or woman sets out to kill someone, they make a good job of it. This is especially true of the *crime passionnel* which is accorded special status in France, passion being perfectly acceptable as a defence, while in England passion might count as a mitigating plea, and in some cases could well count against you.

Government and Bureaucracy

The French like government intervention in their lives. In their eyes, the State not only has a role to play in the everyday life of the country, the State *is* France (as are cooking, wine, women, the land, Paris, culture, children, liberty-equality-fraternity, and the right to park on a pedestrian crossing).

State intervention is something to be proud of, not something to avoid. By the side of French roads huge placards proclaim the partnership between the state, the region and the department which has paid for the improvements. Their tube system is a monument to state planning – it is flawlessly integrated, the Métro linking with the main railway, linking in turn with the Aéroport Charles de Gaulle.

As soon as the technology existed the French put it to use. There is little sense of 'We know we can do it, but can we afford it?' Instead, they believe that if they can do it, they must make sure they can afford it.

All this means that bureaucracy flourishes in France – in post offices, railway stations, customs sheds, town halls, tourist offices, gendarmeries, schools.

The way the French deal with it is to accept that it is necessary, and indeed proper, but find ways to circumvent it. The French have always affirmed their right to disagree with rules (which are always 'petty' if they disagree with them).

Politics

The current French Constitution was drafted in the knowledge that a lurch towards tyranny afflicts France once every generation. This is counterbalanced by a delight in playing with democracy and having lots and lots of tiny political parties, who represent small farmers, small shopkeepers, small fishermen.

Most of these parties have a mayfly existence, fluttering around the National Assembly for a few weeks or months until they crash out of existence.

The cunning safeguard against extremes is that, whereas the president is elected for seven years, the members of the National Assembly are elected for only five years. This means that there are bound to be times, as currently, when their president and parliament are out of step – a situation the French quaintly call 'cohabitation'.

Only the French would take such pains to build confusion and complication into their Constitution.

With subliminal awareness of their deep internal anarchy, the French rigidly respect officialdom but hate officials. Thus the President of France must be accorded full honours, rituals, escorts of motorbikes, and so on, but it is not necessary to value him as a person.

France may no longer be a world power of the first significance, but French politicians show no signs of behaving as though that were true. They take no notice of the world's outrage at their plan to resume nuclear tests on the Mururoa Atoll. Only a truly great nation could possibly have so many enemies.

The French like their politicians to be bold and visionary. They can forgive any mistake or misdemeanour if it is big enough. (It is one of the unwritten laws of the French Constitution that each new government should reveal an appalling scandal perpetrated by the one before.)

All French politicians are also expected to look smart, whatever their shape or age. Even de Gaulle, with his immense height and girth, took pains to avoid the 'sack of potatoes' look of so many English MPs and ministers. French politicians look smart because power itself is chic, attractive, seductive, and one should dress to look the part. The French electorate would never allow any government to intervene in their lives if it were shabbily dressed.

As to the private lives of their representatives, the French cannot understand the problem other nations have when their politicians are discovered engaged in a sexual liaison. It is expected that all male French politicians have mistresses or lovers. Indeed, once a French politician is known to have a lover, he or she can count on more votes.

Business

The French have mastered the art of invisible work. Whereas some nations parade the sweat and grime of industrial and constructional life, the French keep all this hidden. It is as though having to work is incompatible with the notion that the French have discovered the secret of the good life.

They take their work seriously, and conduct it in the formal manner which dictates every aspect of their lives. Behind the scenes (jackets off, ties undone, Gauloise on the lip), all may be friendly and informal.

But in the front office even if they had been calling each other by their first names for decades, etiquette dictates that they call each other 'Monsieur X', 'Madame Y'. The French use 'Monsieur' in conversations in the workplace in much the same way that the English used 'Sir' fifty years ago: "Did you know, Monsieur, that…"

And every morning French business colleagues have to shake hands with each other. Everything must be right and proper before any attempt can be made to work.

Once work is underway, there is a lot of good sense in French practice. Reports within an office as to how well a member of staff is performing, are compiled not only by the subject's line manager or seniors, but also by the employees on the lower rungs of the ladder, who have a different but important perspective on performance.

There are, however, some strange aspects to the way they recruit their office staff. Graphology is regarded as an essential assessment tool. If a French person takes a dislike to your handwriting he may well cancel appointments with you, may even refuse to employ you. The French see graphology as a fully-fledged science, revealing character (or lack of it). Secretly, they must bless the invention of the word processor.

Time Keeping

Despite their strong belief in protocol, manners, and the proprieties of life, the French are almost always late for work, appointments, interviews, etc. They have their own special idea of what constitutes being 'on time'. It means 'being within 15 minutes of the appointed hour'. In their eyes, therefore, they are never late.

Decision Making

Sit a group of British managers down to solve a problem and they will make an honest attempt, eventually coming up with a solution, no matter how unsuitable. Faced with the same problem, French managers will enjoy the discussion, move smartly off at several tangents, and end up with a totally new problem to discuss, to their great satisfaction.

The Way it's Done

The sense of propriety among business colleagues means that they very rarely invite each other home to dinner, or for a drink. The idea of inviting someone from the office for a casual glass of wine, in casual clothes, is unthinkable. Indeed, the French don't really have a word for 'casual'. The nearest they get to it is *sans-gêne*, literally 'without constraint'.

The uniform business suit is not commonly worn to work. They dress with the same flair and imagination that accompanies all that they do. Jackets and trousers of bright and unusual designs and colours (even in banks) are the rule, and dress is no indication of status in the

French business world.

This does not mean that they are not all intensely conscious of whose outfit is the smartest, the most stylish. Egalité may rule, but some are more égal than others.

Women now account for some 45% of the French workforce, but few are to be found in the key positions in industry and big business – despite their high profile in politics from time to time.

Small Business

The romantic and inaccurate view of the French is that they are a nation of entrepreneurs – small blacksmiths, small builders, small notaires. It was widely held that, if a motorist broke down in the most remote French village, the local blacksmith would be able to repair the car, even if it meant hammering out a new carburettor from a chunk of solid metal.

Small businesses are increasingly the exception rather than the rule in France. The French are happy to accept the notion of the large company, for the large company can afford vision and experimentation. It is far more glamorous and thus give its workforce a feeling notoriety. French workers have a pride in their job because they are aware of what they are giving to the community and to France.

The Workers, United

On the whole, the French don't believe in trade unions. Only 8-9% of the workforce are members (compared with 51% in Britain), and the figure falls steadily year by year.

This lack of interest boils down to two things: that

French people don't like joining anything, and that the main unions are usually in dispute with each other (an 'us and us', rather than an 'us and them' problem).

French industry is run by cunning, imaginative men (and one or two women) who make work seem a pleasant interlude between morning coffee and evening apéritifs. They put rest-rooms into their offices and factories, establish flexi-time, allow workers to take a few minutes break whenever they need to, and even let them finish work for the week on a Thursday if they've already reached their productivity targets.

Trade unions wither in the face of such unfair and reasonable onslaughts.

Obsessions

To the French there is little point in living unless one is obsessed. They are obsessed with the Tour de France, the state of their health, the National Lottery, the bac, the meaning of life, barricades and revolutions, and all that is inherently theirs.

Watch the way they play boules – the muttering through the Gitanes, the peering through half-shut eyes, the wiping of sweat from the brow (only the French could break into a muck sweat simply by throwing a small metal ball in the air), the grunting of joy or rage as the point is won or lost, the handshakes all round at the end of every three minute game.

If an innocent pastime can produce such dedication, then what of codes of honour, truth, patriotism, duty and the correct temperature at which to thicken a sauce?

Conversation

The French butt in on each other's conversations. This is not rudeness, but proof that they are listening to what is being said and are sufficiently interested to want to take part. If the interruption takes the form of something along the lines of "Je m'en fous" ("I couldn't care less") then rudeness is intended, and it might be wiser to withdraw as politely as possible.

What passes for normal attempts at conversation among other people may be perceived as bad manners by the French. The stock opening conversational gambits ("What do you do for a living?", "How much do you make?", "Are you married?", and "Do you have any children?") are regarded by the French as none of your business. Better instead to talk about art, culture or, best of all, politics.

Everyone in France has views on these subjects – even the plumber who comes to mend a burst pipe will be happy to discuss Voltaire with you while eating his lunch.

Taboo Subjects

Never mention the War, and, above all, don't bring up the subject of the Occupation – the French didn't enjoy it then and they still don't now. The German march into Paris in June 1940 and the subsequent years of occupation were dreadful blows to pride, patriotism and prestige.

The French do not accept that they were defeated and don't wish to share with others the fact that the Pétain Government in Vichy saved a little of their self-respect, a little of their independence, but at the expense of most of their honour.

Gestures

The French invented body language. To watch a gendarme on traffic control is to witness an elaborate modern ballet – the twirling baton, the palm of the hand thrust forward to bring hundreds of vehicles to a halt, the abrupt inclination of the head that allows them to proceed, the raising of the judgmental eyebrow if all is not in order.

In conversation, French hands are never still. They give shape, form and size to ideas. They display the state of the mind, heart and soul of the parties involved.

Where others use the inflection of the voice to show how they feel, the French use eyes, hands, lips and shoulders to reveal a full range of emotions. They kiss the tips of their fingers when they approve strongly of something or somebody. They pull the hand across the forehead, as though scalping themselves, when they are fed up. They raise their shoulders when confronted by the ridiculous. They stroke their cheeks with the back of the hand as a sign that they are bored. They purse their lips and exhale when they are exasperated.

They have signs for disapproval, incredulity, superiority, apology, amazement, surprise, bewilderment and frustration.

Which is why it is considered grossly impolite to talk with one's hands in one's pockets.

Trading Insults

The French are very good at insults, seen at their best in city rush hour confrontation. They have a rich language for expletives and a lively imagination.

Without knowing a word of French, it is possible to know that you have been insulted, for the French present their insults dramatically, making full use of the grimace and the ugly gesture.

They have dozens of words for the unmentionable, but tend to concentrate on only one or two. 'Connard' and 'con' are routine insults (the latter once held extremely vulgar but now used routinely in conversation). The more prudish may not use the word as such, but spell it out 'c....o....n'.

It can be translated acceptably as 'bloody fool'.

Language and Ideas

The French language is what binds the French together. In the old days, France was divided into regions which spoke different tongues like Breton, Languedoc, Flemish. Almost every area had its own patois. This was seen as a threat to French unity, and in French schools any child who spoke the forbidden patois was given a bean. The bean passed from miscreant to miscreant during the day, and, at the end of the day, the child in possession of the bean was caned.

No other nation has fought so hard to preserve its language. An entire academy (the Académie française) works ceaselessly to ensure its purity, examining every word to make sure it is acceptable. New words which have crept into use are ruthlessly plucked out.

The fad of franglais, common a few years ago, has almost run its course. In business and technical terminology 'le cash-flow', 'le design', 'le pipeline' appalled Mitterrand: "Must we give orders to our computers in English?" he demanded.

An attempt was made to render franglais unnecessary by simply creating French substitutes. 'Un oil-rig' became 'un appareil de forage en mer'. The attempt was quickly abandoned.

When de Gaulle died, Noel Coward was asked what he thought the good General and God would find to talk about in Heaven. Coward replied: "That depends on how good God's French is."

Words to the World

The linguistic bequest of the French to the world has been indispensable. What sort of romance could be conducted without a tête-à-tête, a rendezvous with the right ambiance, a frisson or two, some badinage, the odd nuance and some risquée repartee?

What sort of a war could anyone conduct without sabotage, manoeuvres, the odd massacre, many and frequent mêlées, bags of esprit de corps, a little espionage, liaison, and ultimately détente?

What sort of poise could anyone achieve without being suave and soigné? What sort of political excitement could there be without coups d'état, laisser-faire, faits accompli, volte-face and carte blanche?

How could we show we were out of our milieu if we couldn't make gaffes and faux pas to show that we were thoroughly gauche?

What would we eat in a restaurant, buffet, or café without casseroles, fricassées, hors-d'oeuvres, soufflés, vols au vent, escalopes, consommés, pâté, terrines, éclairs, croissants, omelettes, gâteaux, mousses, sauces....?

And wouldn't everything be passé were it not for the avant-garde?

The Authors

Nick Yapp spent his first night in France in a hay barn near Calais in 1961. Since then he has fallen in love with the French for their music, wine, space, and those purple onions you can't get in England. He fears their driving and is bewildered by the speed at which they speak.

When he sits outside a café in the centre of a small French town on a sunny day, nerves jangling with the first sip of hot, strong coffee, watching the world go by, he feels he has somehow made a success of life. When he gets the bill and sees what this success has cost him, a little of the euphoria evaporates – but he returns the next day.

He used to be a teacher, but escaped to become a writer and broadcaster. In his dreams he lives in a beautiful Basque villa on the clifftops south of Biarritz. In reality, he lives in Catford.

Michel Syrett, French on his mother's side, studied in Paris and now visits France regularly as a business commentator, lecturer and international journalist, contributing to *The Times, The Financial Times*, etc. Being half French has not detracted from the success of his books on leadership.

He speaks French better than he might otherwise because he has found that the way to command attention in the monde of French business, is to eulogise about the style with which the Nuits St. George seductively cohabits with the 'microbes' of the fromage while at the same time making a seriously intellectual evaluation of the pâté de foie gras.